Belle is a beautiful young maiden.
She goes shopping in the village
where she lives.

One day Belle takes a long walk.
She finds a castle in the woods.

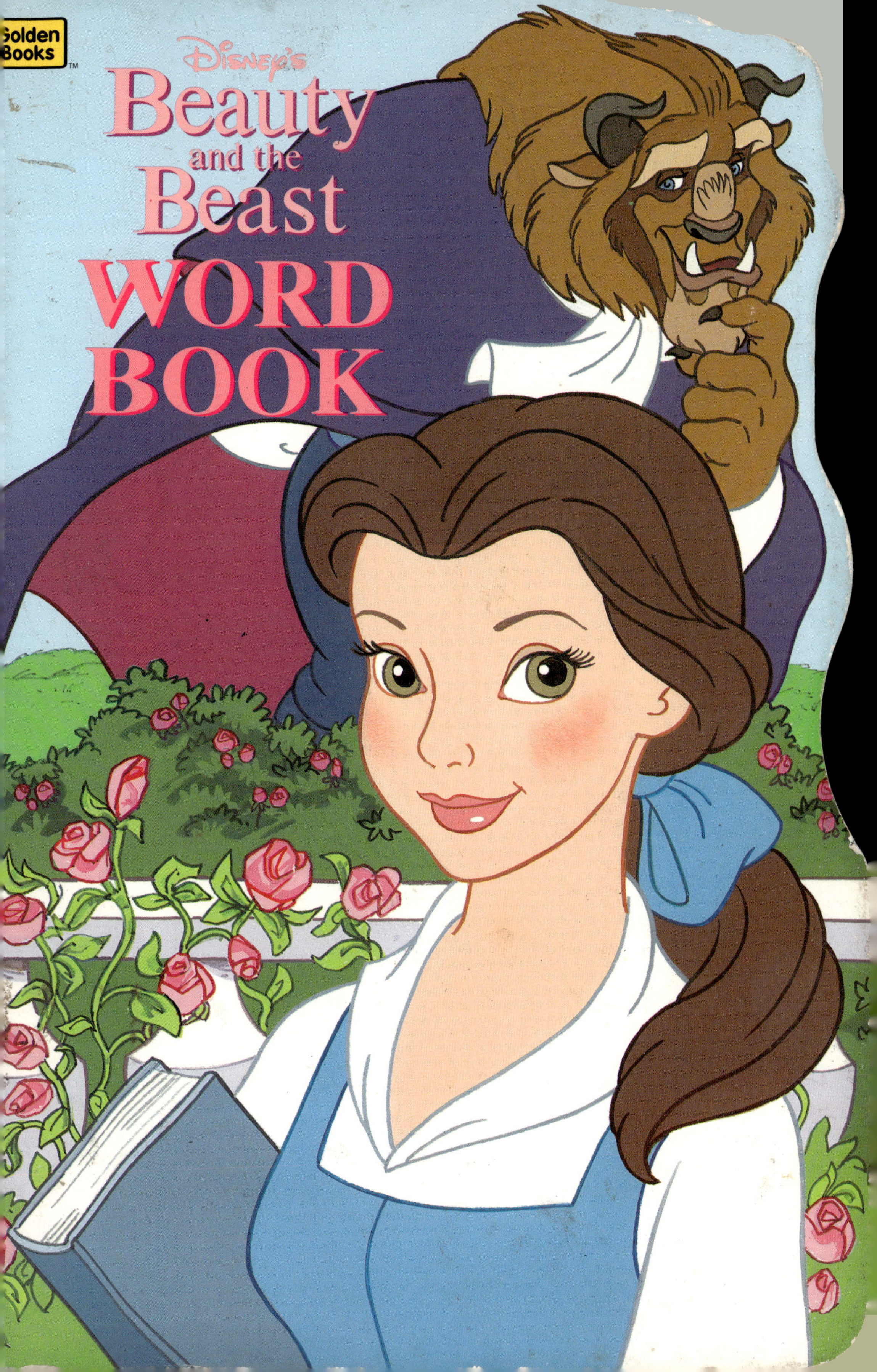
Golden Books
Disney's
Beauty and the Beast
WORD BOOK

A GOLDEN BOOK • NEW YORK
Western Publishing Company, Inc., Racine, Wisconsin 53404

Library of Congress Catalog Card Number: 91-73922 ISBN: 0-307-12391-X
MCMXCVII

stone wall
tree
vine
gate

statue
fireplace

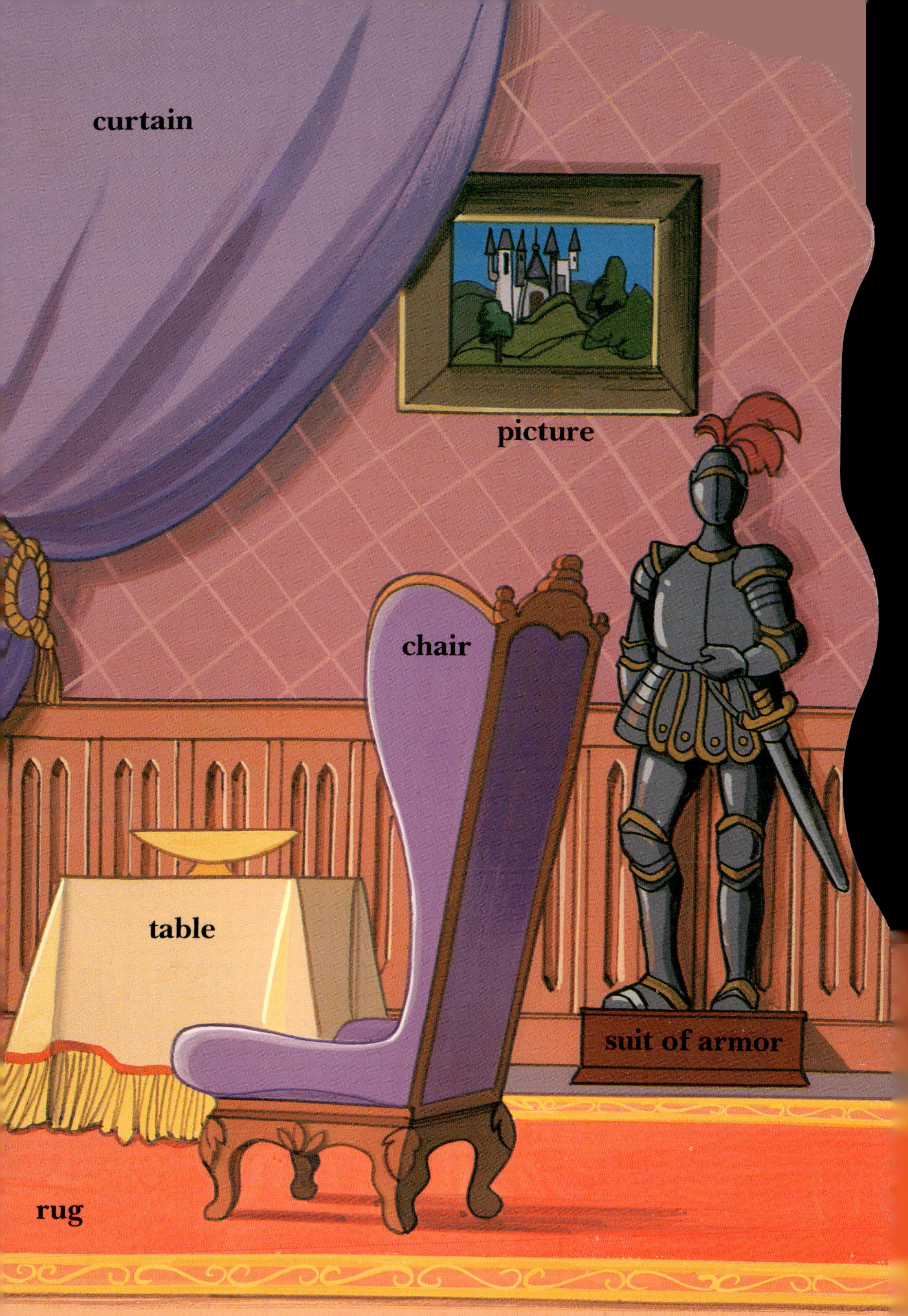

Belle explores the gloomy castle.

plate
napkin
teapot
spoon
fork
footstool

In the castle kitchen,
Belle makes some funny
new friends.

Belle meets the Beast who lives in the castle. Slowly she teaches the Beast to be kind and gentle.

snowflakes
squirrel
snow

tower
cook
boy
door
happy servants
roses

Belle and the Beast fall in love.
And when they kiss, the Beast
turns into a handsome prince.

A GOLDEN STURDY SHAPE BOOK®

Written by Barbara Bazaldua
Illustrated by Darrell Baker

0 33500 12391 7

ISBN: 0-307-12391-X